God at Work

by

Ann Lovett Baird

Scripture quotations are from:

The Holy Bible, New King James Version
©1979,1908,1982 by Thomas Nelson, Inc.
Used by permission.
All rights reserved.

New American Standard Bible®
Copyright © 1960,1962,1963,1968,1971,1972,
1973,1975,1977,1995 by the Lockman Foundation.
Used by permission.
(www.Lockman.org)

The Holy Bible, King James Version

Cover design by: Jeff Morrison

Published by:
Lovett Press International
214-350-1696
ann@lovettconsulting.com

Dedication

I dedicate this book to my parents, Thomas and Johnnye Jean for their unfailing love for me. Their devotion to our Lord Jesus Christ has always served as a motivation for my deepening faith and walk with the Lord.

I also dedicate this book to my daughters. I see God at work in them every day.

Acknowledgments

Thank you to Alan Rich, whose insightful suggestions made the manuscript richer. And thanks to my friend who asked that her name not be mentioned. Her suggestions made the book cleaner.

I also thank my Dad, Thomas P., for being a constant advisor for scriptural reference while I was writing this book.

Introduction

I left corporate America because I felt God was bidding me to another chapter in my life as a businessperson. Almost sixteen years after starting my consulting practice, I feel it's more appropriate to call it our consulting practice, because the Lord has always been by my side every step of the way. What an opportunity we have in our work to witness for the Lord by our actions, our lives and our belief in miracles anywhere, including the workplace. Sometimes this means choosing between acting according to the principles we live by as Christians, and following the desires of corporate powers. God is always at work when we are ready to notice Him, and, He does work miracles in the workplace.

God at Work is meant to inspire Christians in their walk with Christ in the workplace. I prayerfully hope that God will use these pages to inspire workers in their daily toils, no matter what their position, task or situation.

Ann Lovett Baird
2011

Table of Contents

God is Building a House

God is constantly building a house. God's workings in the workplace can be likened to building a house. Houses need a firm foundation, set on rock or reinforced so that the foundation won't shift. Our faith and values in the workplace can't shift, even when they are challenged. The house that God builds sits on a firm foundation, not shifting sand. If we follow the teachings of Jesus Christ, and walk by faith with Him, our work life will be built on a firm foundation, which will support us in the daily trials of corporate life.

"Therefore, whoever hears these sayings of mine, and does them, I will liken him to a wise man who built his house on the rock: and the rain descended, the floods came, and the winds blew and beat on the house; and it did not fall for it was founded on the rock."

—Matthew 7:24-25, New King James Version

(NKJV)

Many houses have a wooden frame, surrounded by sheet rock, insulation, windows and doors. If the frame is faulty, no matter how beautiful the brick on the outside is, the house will not stand. The same is true of our stand for God and integrity, or Christian principles in the workplace. We can look great on the outside, go to church, live honestly at work, but if the inside of our framework of faith is not unshakeable, our house will not stand the tide of the working world. So many opportunities for greed, stepping on people to get ahead, or saying boastful things to make us look good present themselves daily. If we give in to these temptations they will weaken the framework of standing for our Lord in the corporate world.

I once had a boss tell me that I agreed with people in other departments too much. The idea of not building positive relationships with people was totally foreign to me. This man was a devout churchgoer and proud of it. I'm sure he even contributed money and time to the church. Yet, his motives in business did not appear to reflect how

Christ has commanded Christians to live. Often I watched him attack others or other departments, either openly or secretly in order to gain power and get his own way. He had his sights on a certain management position that was held by someone else. I watched for two years as he gradually worked away at the man who had the position he wanted, questioning his judgment at every public opportunity. In staff meetings for our department he would badmouth other departments and what they were doing. He did not demonstrate Christian values in the workplace.

The framework of what we stand for in terms of faith ultimately affects what shows on the outside. Just as the creaky floor in an upstairs bedroom in my home demonstrates that the house may need more support from the frame, eventually a shaky framework of faith will show through to the outside.

Builders use a blueprint to make sure they build houses to specification. Without the plan, the door and the window might be put in the wrong place. Without a logical construction schedule, tasks might be completed in the wrong order. For example, the carpet would be laid before the paint was complete, or the bathroom would be put in before the plumbing was complete. God has a plan for how our life goes too. Homes are not built in a day, just as our growth as Christians walking in faith does not happen all at once. Our relationship with God deepens over time. There is a definite decision to follow Christ and accept Him as savior; that is the first step on a journey with Him. Sometimes the journey takes us to places we don't want to go. Just as, sometimes in our working lives, we have to do things that are uncomfortable on the surface, but the right things to do. Maybe we have to tell clients we are not available because the meeting they scheduled conflicts with an important family event. We might have to back away from something or a project if we feel it is immoral or unethical. Some business relationships might have to be severed because the outcome and by-products of them does not glorify the Lord.

The roof, insulation and sheetrock of a house serve as protection from the elements. In the same way the armor of God can protect us in the workplace. He can provide that covering we need to keep us safe from negative forces in the workplace. We have to have faith that our sword of prayer is much swifter and mightier than any words or maneuvering we make in our human effort to fix things. The sword of prayer is not meant to cut down and devastate others in the organization, merely disarm them without harming them. In the martial art of Aikido, the master attempts to disarm his opponent by using the opponent's energy or strength. By not resisting an opponent, the Aikido master throws the foe off-guard. But when the Aikido master gains the upper hand, he does not take advantage of his adversary and beat him up. He merely disarms the adversary to protect himself. The same goes for spiritual warfare in the workplace.

One time, I taught a training class where the participants seemed to really enjoy themselves and gain a lot from the session. Some of the people on the committee responsible for the training were in the room. One person complained because he did not agree with the techniques I was teaching. Some of the committee members came up to me at break and told me a few things they wanted me to change, which were not in my original plan. This was the first in a two-part training series. Between the two sessions, the committee met with me in something that felt similar to the Spanish Inquisition. After the meeting, I was to have another individual meeting with someone on the committee. I prayed for that meeting for several days beforehand.

The meeting went extremely well and the man, who was on the training committee said, "I just want you to do what you do best, because I know you are very good at it, and I will back you 100 percent. I think we were wrong to try to jump in there and change what you were doing because we could not see that the end result was going to be."

I left his office and got in my car praising the Lord, because I know He was in that meeting. Between sessions, I also prayed for every member of the class, that each one would gain something valuable that would help them in their jobs.

A house has windows to let God's light in; just as there are always opportunities in our work to show God's love. More than once I have had a client notice that I am flexible to work with. If the truth be known, it isn't me, but my Heavenly father who is flexible. My ability to be flexible is directly related to the fact that I believe, no matter what, that God will take care of my family and me. So if a project is postponed or cancelled, I know that it is for the best and that God will provide other work. If a client loses an invoice, which delays payment, I understand, because I know that ultimately my life is in God's hands. In every work situation I have the opportunity to demonstrate my faith in God even if I don't overtly say anything to the client. In this way I can serve as a window to the light of God. In the workplace we can shine as something unique and different, as God's light to the world.

> *"Let your light so shine before men,*
> *that they may see your good works and*
> *glorify your Father in heaven."*
> —Matthew 5:16, NKJV

No house is perfect. At one time I lived on a street where some houses are being built. As I took my morning walk, I loved to look at the different houses, notice the façade on this one, the columns on the next, the beautiful trees on the lot of the next one. I began comparing these houses to mine thinking each one was a little better, but, then I would notice something that I really did not like about that house and realize that my house was fine. Ultimately, I came to the conclusion that no house is perfect. As no house is perfect, no company, no job, no friendship is perfect. Only God is perfect and He can use our imperfection to show His glory.

One job had such a bad political climate that I decided to leave. The job wasn't perfect, but it wasn't a mistake that I worked there either. I made very strong friendships that are still strong six years later. These friendships have been the key to the survival of my business.

Thankfully, when a builder builds a house, he uses a plan, a blueprint. The average person wouldn't understand a blueprint, just as we don't always understand God's plan. The blueprint ensures that the house functions like a home; God's plan ensures that we use the gifts, talents and blessings that He bestows on us. As we must trust the builder to build a house that has a kitchen, bathrooms, windows and doors in the right places, we must have faith that God has the blueprints even though we don't always understand His plan. In many cases if life had gone the way I wanted it to, I would not have been as blessed. God knows what I need better than I do. His plan is ultimately so much grander than anything I could ever dream of.

God's Blueprints

An unnerving phenomenon with owning a small
business comes when you look at your calendar and
there are far too many white spaces on it. You
wonder how in the world you will keep the doors
open, how will the business survive, whether God is
really concerned with my financial security? And,
what about the poor soul in the corporation reeling
from corporate down-sizing, merger and acquisition
and re-organization? There, one's future is in the
hands of corporate attorneys, investors and the
bottom line. In that situation, there may be two
employees of equal ability when only one is needed.
Insignificant differences may tell who stays on and
who gets to look for another job.

God has the blueprints, yet sometimes we spill
coffee on them by trying to help God along. We
have to follow in blind faith, knowing He will take
care of us and He will guide us if we let Him. A
house framer nails the boards according to the
architect's plan, trusting that it is correct. The

framer may not totally understand the big picture of how the house will look when it's finished, but he trusts that the creator of the blueprints knew what he was doing. Our magnificent and almighty creator has a plan that we so often question. If we could simply follow God's blueprint, where we believe He is leading, our lives would be so much simpler and less confusing. We can only know what's on His blueprint by asking for direction rather than giving God instructions. Hearing God takes slowing down and listening during prayer time, or asking others to pray for direction. God will provide us direction when we are ready to slow down and listen to Him, or submit to His desires. Following His direction sometimes feels like jumping into a lake without knowing how deep it is, or what lurks below the surface. Only with God, the end result will be the right path. It's not always an easy path, and often has rough spots and craggy turns, but in the end, we can look back at the path, and see how God's hand has crafted every curve. It's like looking back over the countryside to see the country lane twist, turn and finally disappear over the horizon.

A colleague and I were talking about how God was urging me to finish the manuscript for *God at Work.* I told her I was scared because writing a book would keep me from marketing for consulting work that would put money in the bank sooner than the book manuscript. I asked her to pray against my fear so that I would complete the task of writing the book. I knew in my deepest heart that God would take care of my financial needs because He always does. She described a time about six months prior when she had just gotten out of the hospital and had the same fear. When we talked, it was January, and she had just completed one of the most prosperous months in business. Some would call this a great feat since many clients are more focused on events, and year-end activities rather than hiring outside consultants. Toward the conclusion of our conversation, she said, "God has the plans, even when we think we are in control of the business." When I start thinking that I don't need God's help, I get boastful about what I can achieve. Sometimes God has to remind me that all my abilities, gifts, talents and resources come from Him and He has a plan for me. Without His hand managing the blueprint, I am lost.

When we give God the blueprints, He will build a house that is magnificent in its splendor, sturdy at its foundation, hand-crafted with the skill of a gifted artisan. He's got the plan. In Fresh Wind, *Fresh Fire,* Jim Cymbala recounts the story of the birth of the Brooklyn Tabernacle in New York City. A theme early on in the book is that Cymbala and his wife do not have the formal training in seminary and music school; this makes them totally dependent on God and His Holy Spirit. Because they are so dependant, God can use them to glorify Him in grandiose ways. Wouldn't it be terrific if we could turn every business meeting over to the Lord? We might have some very interesting meetings!

A speaker colleague of mine says a prayer prior to every speech she makes, and she has been speaking for over twenty years. The prayer goes like this: "May the words of my mouth and the meditations of my heart be always acceptable to You, oh Lord."

God has truly used her to bless thousands of people in the business world. God has given her a rich and unique gift for speaking and she takes the opportunity to bring God into every speech.

God had a plan for my career. When I was in college I planned for a career in banking. After all, my great granddaddy and great uncle had started a bank in a small Texas town…almost 100 years before. In college, I earned a business degree in Accounting and Finance. I worked in a bank during two summers in college to get some experience. When I graduated, I went back to the bank where I had worked for two summers and got a full-time job. After all, banking was in my family, I had a good head for business and worked well with people. I stayed in the banking business, quite miserably, for nine years, until I was laid off by a struggling bank.

When I lost that job, I remembered feeling like a miserable failure. The world felt like it was crashing in, and yet it was all part of God's plan. My experience in banking has definitely helped me in business. My knowledge of finance and accounting has been crucial to the success of my consulting firm. After my time as a commercial banker, I spent three years in the mortgage business working on a commission basis. That experience helped me in training and inspiring salespeople, which is currently a key focus of my business. After commercial banking and the mortgage business, I finally landed in professional speaking and training, a vocation God had groomed me for all along.

I know that as I move forward in my life, God will show me other ways that I can use my experience and education to glorify Him and provide for my family. Through my business experience I have honed my writing, speaking and facilitation skills, all of which contribute to what I do for my clients.

For many years I thought I was a little strange because I would think of so many analogies in life to make a point. When I started out as a corporate trainer, these analogies came in handy to help explain concepts. In a National Speaker's Association seminar that I attended once, the speaker told us about a method of writing a speech in which you make a point and tell a story to demonstrate the point. I love to write, so suddenly I realized how my writing and love of writing stories could help me make compelling speeches. Many gifted and seasoned speakers actually write the speech down and memorize it very carefully, so the delivery and message are more powerful. It seems that God has been preparing me for this work for a long time.

God's blueprint is woven like a tapestry of people, events and relationships that we can't always see. When I started as a trainer for a Texas-based Savings and Loan I got involved in The American Society for Training and Development (ASTD), a professional organization for Human Resources Development professionals (aka trainers, corporate training managers and training designer types). In that organization I served as the program chairman one year. A speaker, who served on a panel for one of the programs that year, and I became good friends. She had been a training manager for a large regional bank for a number of years until she started her own training consulting firm. For several years before I started my training consulting company, I knew I wanted to go out on my own, but wasn't quite sure how. Several times my friend offered me opportunities to do some contracting work for her, but it was never enough to lure me from the corporate safety net. Then, in 1995, she made an offer I couldn't refuse. I spent six months writing banking courses for one of her clients. It was a terrific opportunity, and, as a bonus, my work was closely edited by a consultant who worked for my friend. My editor sharpened my writing skills, which had gotten sloppy during the years of cranking out training fast and alone in the corporate workplace.

I thank God that He has the blueprints. If I had not lost the job as a bank lender many years ago, I might never have used the gifts and talents that God gave me. Some of my most difficult times in life come when I don't want to give up the plans. My peace has always come when I let go, accept, and thank God for things the way they are and follow what I feel God is calling me to do.

If you are trying to take charge of the blueprints in your life, try giving them back to God. You'll be amazed at how much lighter you will feel and what a masterful hand God has in making the plans.

The Foundation

"And whoever does not bear his cross
and come after Me cannot be My
disciple. For which of you, intending to
build a tower, does not sit down first
and count the cost, whether he has
enough to finish it-lest, after he has had
laid the foundation, and it not able to
finish, all who see it begin to mock him
saying, 'This man began to build and
was not able to finish.'"

—Luke 14:27-30, NKJV

Sometimes carrying the Lord into the workplace
means bearing our cross. Not always an easy task
and impossible without a very strong commitment
to being a disciple for Christ. Being a disciple for
Christ and living daily with Him create a value
system in us that is challenged, yet not shaken. It
means living our life before Him, even when no one

else is looking. The man who builds the tower knows he must have a foundation sturdy enough to hold the rest of the structure, and the ability to complete the entire building project. If we leave our Christian values at home when we ride the train, hop the bus or fight rush hour traffic to get to the office, then, we cannot finish the job the Lord has for us in the workplace. When we lay the foundation, we have to finish the work. Finishing the work means setting a good example, and interacting with people in a way that honors God.

I know of a businessman who was in a situation where he had every right to sue an entity for non-performance on a contract. Yet rather than pursue legal action, he went to God to solve the problem. This takes great faith in the business world, but imagine how much more would get accomplished if we all depended on God to iron out our differences. Supporting a family, running a business, doing everything the boss requires is a challenge…but not a challenge too big for God. If we honor Him, He will honor us.

God the Business Consultant

God created the universe and everything in it, so why don't we turn to Him for advice on running our businesses? One time I was proposing to do work for a firm in Dallas. I worked up the proposal, figured the number of hours it would take to complete the project and put a price on the proposal. Then I worried that I would not get the work. I thought I should lower the price, but kept feeling like God was telling me to raise it.

Then I started debating with God: "Are you sure? I really need this work."

Finally, I priced the project as God directed. When I met with the client to present the proposal, she cruised through the it quickly and got to the back where the price was listed and exclaimed, "This is cheap!"

I was so truly amazed at how God, who created the universe, magnificent in His power and glory, cared about me enough to reveal to me something I could not have known about my potential client. God always is there to give me direction in my business if I will only stop and listen.

Another time, my business was suffering badly. I had only one client. The one project was so time-consuming that I stopped making the time to try to get additional projects or business to keep my consulting firm afloat. I prayed about this every day and started thinking I should try to find an 8:00 to 5:00 job. Every time I prayed, I felt God was telling me to hang in there with the consulting practice. I felt like God knew that the business was going to change, that I just had to trust Him. I had to step out in faith and continue trusting that God would not forsake my family and me. I had several discussions with the Lord regarding how much money was in my checking account. I continued to get very strong indications from the Lord that I could not see what was going to happen to the business in the months ahead. I continued to contact people who I knew in the training world and build relationships with colleagues and potential clients.

Finally, on a Sunday afternoon, I said, "Okay Lord, this is it. I can't do this anymore."

I felt the Lord promised that the very next day, things would change. The next day passed very quietly. My office was silent except for the clacking of my computer keyboard and the purring of the computer fan, as I tried to write something for the one small client I had. It was all quiet on the consulting front…until about 4:30 in the afternoon. The phone rang. It was a potential client who needed some consulting work done. In the course of an hour, three clients called me with work they wanted me to do. And, these people were sure I was the one they wanted to do the work. They did not want a proposal to bid against other consultants. It was almost as if God had told each of them. You know, you need to call Ann Baird, she's the perfect one for this project. The next year and a half was extremely profitable for my tiny consulting firm. Only two-and-a-half years after I left a bank to start my own company, I had a net income of almost twice the amount I was making on salary.

God, the business consultant, knew that for a small business like mine to survive, constantly building relationships and marketing were key to keeping it alive. All the relationship-building I did during that slow time really paid off. The bonus was the fact that these strong relationships allowed me to share God's love with people in a working environment. His love inside of me is what people wanted to work with. My skill and talents, the way I look, the way I act are just the shell. God on the inside is what really matters to people, even when they don't know it.

Building relationships with people so I can share my faith with them and they can feel God's love is like me finishing the building where I have laid a foundation. When people know what I stand for I have even more of a calling to live according to Christ's path for me. A firm foundation helps me to stay focused on Him in spite of what may be happening around me in the workplace. For in living His life in the workplace, I witness for God in a way that is much louder than anything I can say.

You can finish your tower by walking with and beside people in the workplace so that they can see God in you and see how He helps you deal with life's challenges. We can witness for God through our attitude toward things that happen to us. Even though a burden doesn't appear light, with God at our side, the burden is an easy load. The burden feels light because God has given us splendid peace and rest for our souls.

> *"Come to Me all you who labor and are*
> *heavy laden, and I will give you rest.*
> *Take My yoke upon you and learn from*
> *Me, for I am gentle and lowly in heart,*
> *and you will find rest for your souls.*
> *For My yoke is easy and My burden is*
> *light."*
>
> —Matthew 11:28-30, NKJV

Values in the Workplace

When our foundation of faith is laid on solid rock, it cannot be shaken by the wiles of corporate life and constant demands. If we are asked to do things that violate our Christian beliefs, we will have the stamina, the courage to stand up for what we know is right. The shifting sands of the business world will not slither under our feet and throw us off-balance. Shifting sands can affect us in our personal lives too. That's why it's so important that we have a solid ground of faith, belief and relationship with Christ to keep us on the solid ground; the sound path of a daily walk as a Christian. When the temptation comes to step on someone to get ahead, to say an ugly word or gossip about someone, to blame others for our mistakes, to decide that the client is all wrong, we can stop and think about what Jesus would have us do. We can leave the shifting sand behind and walk forward toward the light of Christ.

> *"Everyone who comes to Me, and hears My words, and acts upon them, I will show you whom he is like: he is like a man building a house, who dug deep and laid a foundation upon the rock; and when a flood arose, the river burst against that house and could not shake it, because is had been well built. But the one who has heard, and has not acted accordingly, is like a man who builds a house upon the ground without any foundation; and the river burst*

> *against it and immediately it collapsed,*
> *and the ruin of that house was great."*
> —Luke 6:47-49, NASV

Hear the words of our Lord and build your house on solid rock.

Is it right to negotiate the deal to the point of hurting the other party? How does that balance with serving the client who is paying you money? Your boss wants you to make the best deal for the company. It's about overcoming the competition or getting the better deal for your side isn't it? And, when faced with a work situation where you are asked to go against what you believe is right as a Christian, what then? How do you handle that? It may mean saying something uncomfortable and standing up for your beliefs. It might even mean giving up a job or moving to another town. God will never forsake you. He won't leave you stranded when you stand up for Him.

When we walk with Christ our values as Christians must hold firm, because we know we live our lives before Him, not before anyone else, and what we do is a bigger witness for Him than what we say. If we live according to our Christian values we will operate in business life knowing that God is watching us and that we answer to Him. Not that God is a big policeman waiting to punish us, rather, He loves us enough to desire that we don't do things that hurt us or others. And, I don't believe that God calls all of us to wear sackcloth. Financial success is not bad as long as it does not become an idol. God has called all of us who believe in Him to a specific station in life and way of living. Some people may have more power, money or talent than we do, some have less.

We don't need to let people walk all over us either. Negotiating a win-win situation in business may take standing up for our interests or our company. God did not promise that living as a Christian in the world would be easy. This applies especially in the business world.

> *"Behold I send you out as sheep in the midst of wolves; therefore, be wise as serpents, and harmless as doves."*
> —Matthew 10:16, NKJV

As Christians in the workplace, we must be wise, and sometimes give tough messages, yet we should do it in a way that is harmless and kind. I had a client who was teaching associates to sell his product over the telephone. The salespeople for another company that sold the same type of product were saying that my client's product was inferior, which as far as I could observe was not true. My client found this out because when his salespeople would call a potential customer, the customer would say that the "other" company had already called and said that his products were inferior. My client wanted me to write scripts that would deny what the competition was saying without overtly criticizing them. He was consumed with the unfair way the competition was treating him. God gave me the wisdom to see that he was so focused on overcoming the negative press created by his competition that he had lost sight of focusing on potential customers and their needs. I explained, as diplomatically as possible, that he was losing sales by worrying about what the other company was doing wrong, instead of teaching his salespeople to assess potential customers' needs. The salespeople that I worked with were much happier with the needs assessment method of selling because it did not feel manipulative to them. I had to express the wisdom that God gave me in a way that was harmless to the client. He did not feel like I was making him wrong, only that as an outside consultant, I was giving him a different perspective. Ultimately, the environment of the company was more pleasant, and the salespeople were more content with their jobs. I believe God wants our working environments to be emotionally comfortable. Not to say that everything is easy to do and that there are not hard decisions to make, but that working and making those decisions in a more pleasant emotional place creates less stress and happier employees.

Another client of mine needed sales training for branch employees. I visited with several department managers in the organization to determine what they felt the branch employees needed. Then, I went "shopping," posing as a potential customer. I found various ways that the branch employees needed to improve. When branch employees came to training, some of them recognized me. I explained that I had posed as a potential customer in order to determine what skills they needed to improve in order to serve customers better.

Again, God gave me wisdom to go and observe people in the branches and to determine how a customer might feel. I had to deliver the message carefully, so that participants in the training classes would not feel like I was betraying them by "shopping" the branches, and wouldn't rebel to the new skills I was teaching them.

What happens when we feel we have been treated unfairly by a Christian colleague? Does that give us the right to stand up, beat our chest, point the finger and say the person is a dirty rotten scoundrel? Hardly. The one with no sin should cast the first stone. That counts me out. After all, we are all sinners and are allowed into Heaven only by the grace of God through the death of His son on the cross. And, the judgment of the other person will only hold us back and keep us from achieving what God has in mind. God commands us to forgive one another.

> *"And whenever you stand praying, if*
> *you have anything against anyone,*
> *forgive him; that your Father in heaven*
> *may also forgive you your trespasses."*
> —Mark 11:25, NKJV

What's amazing is when we forgive someone, we are freed from the bondage of judgment and hurt. I had a friend who bought an interest in an oil well from someone he went to church with. When my friend made no money on the deal, he realized the person who sold him the interest had misrepresented the surety of return on the investment. My friend spent months dwelling on how bad this man was. He was determined to bring the wrong-doer out into the light. Essentially my friend's anger began to drive his every action. My friend's anger separated him from God. Not only that, this incident drove people away from him because he was so angry and upset.

Really sin is about separation from God and His will. I don't believe that God intends for us to be trapped in a mire of anger and resentfulness. Most of the time we are more hurt by hanging on to those negative feelings that anyone else is. Letting go of feelings of anger and hurt can be very difficult because we expect everything to be fair.

Back in the sandbox when one of our friends took the favorite pail and shovel, perhaps we protested, that it wasn't fair because she used that pail yesterday. Sometimes the things we protest as adults are as trivial. Life isn't always equitable, yet we have God to hold us up when something goes wrong. We have God to depend on when we feel we've been treated unfairly. Why wallow in negative thoughts when it's ours to be joyful in the Lord?

Once I had a client fire me on voicemail. Her words were harsh and she would not return my phone calls. What she said weighed on my pride too. She said I didn't know what customer service meant . . . I pride myself on treating clients well. She attacked my ability to communicate effectively, which was hard to swallow.

What sparked her anger seemed to be a letter that I attached to a draft of training material that I was writing for her. I was trying to go out of town on vacation, and said in a note what I would typically say in person. Obviously, that was a mistake.

I took that letter and asked a friend, who is a writing consultant to review it. I got what I wanted: validation from an expert that my letter and actions were no cause to be fired from the project. For months after that, I replayed what the client said in my head so much that it kept me from getting other business. Oh poor wounded me, I have been treated so unfairly. Enough already. Had I forgiven the harsh words right away and even looked and said, maybe my client's accusations were well-deserved, I could have moved on faster. Pride goes before the fall, and in this case, pride went before falling in a gully!

> *"Pride goes before destruction,*
> *And a haughty spirit before stumbling.*
> *It is better to be of humble spirit with*
> *the lowly,*
> *Than to divide the spoil with the*
> *proud."*
> —Proverbs 16:18-19, NASV

To carry out my mission with that client, to finish building the tower I had begun, I should have written a letter of apology, taking the blame for the miscommunication and moved forward, holding no grudges. Perhaps the client's words were God's nudging me not to be so stubborn. The disagreement we had was really minor, a matter of wording. The client might have even taken me back with a decent apology.

As consultants, I don't believe that we should merely take orders from clients, because they are paying us for our expertise. However, a spirit of humility is good. It keeps us honest and focused on helping the client achieve a goal rather than who is right. God will give us nudgings to help us manage our business lives. We just have to be ready to notice Him.

As a businessperson, following God's advice can clearly make us successful. Having His form of behavior as a basis for all we do keeps us on track, allows us to finish building what we start. Asking Him to guide us daily in our working lives is as important as asking Him to bless our daily personal lives.

The Framework

The difference between a custom home and a home of less quality is often found in the framework and the foundation. I live in a nice house, but it's not a custom home. After living in the house only one year, the ceiling in the den has started creaking when people in the room above walk around. My brother is a custom home builder, and he tells me that the creaking has something to do with the strength and quality of the framework. The strength of a home's framework can make the difference between good and great. A strong framework will stand in spite of the fact that windows are holes in the structure. Windows are holes in the structure, yet they provide natural light to those who dwell inside. They are essential to the natural beauty of a home. For me personally, natural light flowing into a room, whether from a cloudy sky or a clear sunny day, can actually uplift my mood.

The Difference between Good and Great

The difference between good and great seems to be humility. I think of great leaders in the world, and what makes them stand out above good leaders. Often, the difference between them is humility. Consider Russian czars who were overthrown because they did not have the needs of their people at heart. Nelson Mandela spent much of his time in jail, a very humble place, but the people still had him as leader in their hearts. The apostle Paul wrote some of the more joyful passages in the Bible from his humble jail cell. Princess Diana won the hearts of the world by being a representative of the British Royal family who was not afraid to hold hands with people with AIDS. Mother Teresa died essentially penniless, but many a rich and powerful person sought her out for her spiritual counsel. In 1979 she won the Nobel Peace Prize. Mother Teresa was a humble and great steward of God's love and peace in the world.

Some company executives are good leaders but too sure of their autonomy. The truly great leaders in companies have enough humility to realize that they are servant leaders. They know that the more they serve their employees' needs, that the customer, who keeps them in business, will be better served. By listening to the right advisors in the company, they can keep the enterprise on a focused and healthy course.

Jesus gave us the perfect example of how to lead. He made the hard decisions, took the unpopular road more than once, and yet, He was so humble He died an extremely excruciating death for the sake of His followers and all sinners past, present, and future. The son of God and the greatest teacher ever, died in the most humble and painful way. After trekking up a dusty trail, carrying a heavy crossbeam, beaten and exhausted, nails were driven into His hands and feet and He was left hanging to die. He taught people around him with His words and His life.

In the working world, showing humility and love may not be what everyone is doing, but reflecting those characteristics will certainly make us stand out as business people.

> *"Love suffers long and is kind; love does not envy; love does not parade itself, is not puffed up; does not behave rudely, does not seek its own, is not provoked, thinks no evil; does not rejoice in iniquity, but rejoices in the truth; bears all things, believes all things, hopes all things, endures all things."*
>
> —I Corinthians 13:4-7, NKJV

Windows

They say that the eyes are the windows to the soul. I believe that is true, if you notice those around you. The eyes that are steady indicate a person who is secure. Eyes that are piercing or almost accusing could indicate anger. Soft, steady eyes indicate God's gift of mercy, or true understanding from someone. So what do the windows of your soul tell others about your beliefs?

In a home, windows shed light in a house. We have windows that shed light on our faith. In the workplace, we can help people see God and the mercy of Jesus Christ by letting light come through us, like light comes through windows into a home.

Some people suffer from depression due to lack of brilliant sunlight. These people have a difficult time dealing with rainy days or bleak winter days. If people live in a corporation with no light of day or the glory of Christ, the corporate life becomes dank and full of anger, sorrow and stress. We can reflect the beauty of Christ, what He did on the cross as a light to Corporate America.

How can you bring the light of Christ into the workplace? When people observe you in the workplace, do they see someone who acts with kindness, humility, and love? Sometimes bringing the light and love of Christ into the workplace is a challenge. It may be something you really have to work at.

Bricks and Mortar

The bricks and mortar of a house protect those inside from the elements. In the business world, constant elements of greed, unethical behavior or unloving situations confront us daily. While we cannot totally avoid these situations, we can use God's sword of strength and power to protect us. Prayer is one of our most powerful protections against the wiles of the world, whether we are driving down a crowded highway of unfriendly drivers, in a greedy or hostile work environment, or confronted with gossipy neighbors or disrespectful teenagers. What a wonderful tool we have in prayer to protect us and to show our Father in heaven, and those around us, that we have faith in His power. As the bricks protect us from the cold and the heat, our covering of prayer protects us from the things that keep us from focusing on God. And in focusing on God and bringing His love into every situation, we have nothing to fear.

The perfect love of Christ casts out fear. If something goes wrong with a relationship at work, we know that God's perfect love can mend that. Since God has the hairs on our head numbered, wouldn't He see fit to take care of every working situation we have? Our job in our relationship with Him, is to have faith that He will take care of us. Faith is one of the biggest tests and demonstrations of the depth of our relationship with God. If we lose a job, what lesson is He trying to show us, what is He trying to lead us to that is so much better than what we have now? We are armed with the bricks of prayer and the mortar of fearless courage in God's love for us, and His ability and willingness to take care of us.

Prayer Warriors

"Put on the full armor of God, that you may be able to stand firm against the schemes of the devil."
—Ephesians 6:11, NASV

Just as the gatekeeper at my subdivision keeps out people who don't belong there, and might harm the residents, God can protect us from forces at work that defy God and His believers. The gatekeeper can also help the residents if they have difficulty or need assistance getting their access key to work. Without the guard's help, people might not be able to get home.

God can help us in the workplace as the guard helps people get their homes. When we lose our way, maybe by not focusing on what we know God is calling us to do, or we get off track and embroiled in greed or unethical decisions that violate our walk as faithful Christians, Christ can lead us home. He is the unchanging influence in our ever-changing world situation, economy and sometimes chaotic lives.

You may need prayer covering in the workplace. People who have helped me weather life's storms are prayer warriors. These are people who agree to pray with me about certain issues, decisions or challenges. I have asked for prayer support regarding my personal life since I was a teenager. Having prayer warriors in my personal life seems natural so, why not have prayer warriors at work? Why not serve as a prayer warrior at work?

Once a friend told me of a Real Estate deal he was working on that involved an investor who was supposed to give him seed money for a large deal he was working on. The investor was playing power games with the money, promising equity for the deal, then, withdrawing his commitment of funds. I prayed that God would soften the investor's heart. Several weeks later, I learned that the Real Estate deal was actually signed during the time that I was praying for the investor. God will help us in business if we let Him. I believe God would love for us to turn our needs to Him regarding anything we have to do in business.

Another friend was in a business situation that was causing him great stress. He was subleasing office space from someone he had met at church who professed to be a devout Christian. Unfortunately, the landlord created an atmosphere of oppression in the office that seemed to affect everyone. My friend began to see only the negative in the situation and as a result his business began to suffer. One Sunday night we went to his office and prayed for God's spirit to be present, and that the office workers would not feel oppressed. The next day, I prayed all day long that God would convict the landlord of wielding undue control over people in the office. I suggested that my friend thank Jesus for the landlord every time he got upset at him.

At the end of the day, my friend told me that for the first time in many weeks he was able to sit down with the landlord and speak honestly about their arrangement for the office space and business. God's spirit started to work in the hearts of the landlord and my friend to create peace in the workplace.

Once, I was talking with a group of potential clients about delivering some sales training to them. During the meeting, I was talking to the corporate training manager, and two other department heads. I could tell that the corporate training manager was feeling very uncomfortable in the meeting and I sensed that the two mangers were reacting oddly to what I had to say. I asked the group how they would ensure that the people who attended training would use what they learned, and what follow-up activities we should plan. Everyone in the meeting looked at me in bewilderment. Evidently it was something that they had never thought of.

I kept trying to impress them until finally I said a prayer to myself, "God, please take over this meeting."

Out of the blue one of the managers said, "You know your idea about follow-up training is really a good one. We should do that."

When he said that, I sensed an ease of tension with the training manager. The entire mood of the meeting changed in an instant. At the end of the meeting, we went on a tour of these managers' departments. As we were finishing the tour, one of the managers noticed my ring with a cross etched in it.

She smiled and said, "I really like your ring."

We talked briefly about where each of us attended church.

When we parted, she said, "God bless you."

Though it may seem like a small incident, it shows me that all I need to do is invite God to be with me in business situations and He is always glad to be there.

No Fear

"There is no fear in love; but perfect love casts out fear, because fear involves punishment, and the one who fears is not perfect in love."
                              —I John 4:18, NASV

"Do not fear for I am with you;
Do not anxiously look about you, for I am your God.

*I will strengthen you, surely I will help
you.
Surely I will uphold you with My
righteous right hand."*
—Isaiah 41:10, NASV

When I think of the fears that I have, they usually occur because I am not acting on my faith and believing that God is bigger than any problem that I have. Fear is stifling and truly a stumbling block. It is true, as noted in I John, that when I act in perfect love and with God, I have no fear. And as God said to Israel in Isaiah, the Lord is always there to protect me and even fight my battles for me. I do not have to try and slash enemies down with a sword, for God is my most powerful sword.

The fear is a distraction from following God in faith. Faith applies to everything I do…raising children, conducting business and maintaining relationships. Fear takes my focus off of God and wastes valuable time and energy that could be put into more productive activities. Fear makes me doubt that I can use the gifts that God has given me. One thing I have learned is how relationships with people who are driven by fear can pull me down. Trusting God in relationships means I don't need to fear being treated wrongly or unfairly. God can also provide wisdom in choosing relationships that won't be poisoned by fear. Fear stops me from believing I can achieve what God inspires me to achieve. Fear stifles my growth in relationships because my fear prevents me from trusting people. If we truly believe that God is with us, we can trust others, because if people violate our trust we have God to hold us up when we fall.

No fear means that I can let go and let God have control of things. No fear provides freedom to live as God's child in the world without reservation for following where He leads. Having no fear in the workplace sometimes means having no fear regarding how a client will react to an honest opinion or directive from a consultant. If I have to tell a client something I fear they won't like, I might toil over it in my mind for days and nights. When, really what I should do is simply ask God to bring His grace into the situation. If I demonstrate Christ's love in the delivery of a tough message to a client, it would make the situation easier for both of us.

Sometimes when I go to a client for the first time, I pray that God will calm any fears and give me good ears for listening. He can give me insights for how to best serve the client and help the client be more successful. With God working through me, there is no fear in any business situation.

Interior Decorations

The outside of a house doesn't always reflect what is on the inside of the house. The outside of a house might be a traditional red brick, while the inside décor has Southwestern themes. Sometimes companies with a wonderful exterior are not exactly what they present themselves to be.

Before she worked for me, my assistant worked for a company because it was rated one of *Fortune* magazine's best companies to work for. What she discovered was good pay, but not-so-hot working conditions. She told me that she thought the company was a bit cultist. She didn't like the idea that she had to work all day Saturday, then, attend a company meeting on Sunday, which kept her from going to church. What seemed wonderful on the outside, from a credible source like *Fortune* magazine, turned out to be a place where she did not enjoy working. The interior decorations of a company are comprised of various forces, facts and situations. The nice shiny outside view of a company with great pay and benefits, may be that way because it is hard to get employees to stay there.

The unpleasant working environment of some companies may be due to sour relationships in the past or present. An unpleasant working environment can affect you so that you cannot function and you lose focus on performing well. The unfinished business of past or present relationships of people in the company can mean death to productivity and even to a business in some cases. Sometimes a company has some cultural or internal issues that have never been resolved correctly or noticed for that matter.

In some cases you may not be able to control the internal workings of a company, so you have to let go and work around them. There could be a company culture, like the one I experienced at one small financial institution, where everyone was angry and generally distrustful of others. I found that I hated going to work, because I felt so out of control in the situation. I knew there were practices going on that were wrong. I knew some customers were not being treated well. I even let myself be pushed into treating customers in a way that didn't feel right. I was trying to make people in the bank like me, and as a result I violated the very skill or talent I had for maintaining relationships.

If I had given God control, I would have been able to handle the situation better. By trying to control others' negative attitudes and distrust, I lost sight of the value I really brought to the Institution. I didn't even do for the bank what they really wanted me to do, which is to bring in new business.

The bank needed new customers badly. My bringing in new customers might have saved the bank from its demise.

Some of us are called to be Christian soldiers and carry the cross into the workplace even if what we say is unpopular or hard for people to accept. Once, I challenged a boss I had who was digging at another department head by talking about the lack of success of one of their marketing programs. He said something in a department meeting about the performance of bankers in the program that was not true.

In front of the entire 12-person department I responded, almost in shock at what he said, "That's not true."

At the time, I thought I had made a grave error and in fact covered up what I said to make my boss look good. Now, in retrospect, I'm not so sure that what I said was wrong to say. Perhaps God was using me as His warrior, speaking the truth in the workplace.

Unfinished Business

"We project the unfinished business without earthly fathers onto our heavenly Father." I heard a very wise man say that recently.

It struck me as very true. I think about people I know who are still at war with their fathers, even though their earthly fathers have been dead for over ten years. I've seen people ruin relationships, personally and in business because of old garbage they have with their own fathers. That tarnished relationship with earthly fathers that still endures long after the father has left the earth, infiltrates current relationships. The damaged and ugly parts of the father-child relationship can indeed be projected onto our heavenly Father. Our heavenly Father who wants us to love Him so much, can go on existing without a relationship with one human. The real question is, can we go on living without Him.

Letting Go

Be quiet before God at work? HA! Impossible! I start my business day with a daily walk, breakfast, e-mail check, task list review and then "run" as fast as I can to finish everything I need to do in a day. When my business is in trouble, I might ask God what to do.

Until, I realize that I need to stop, ask Him on the morning walk, "What should I do today Lord? How should I proceed, who should I call, what do you want me to do Lord?"

He often answers specifically, to call a certain person or finish a certain project first. He always knows so much better than I do what I should do, yet I think that because He does not have a business degree, God could not possibly help me in business. What I fail to see is how all the business dealings of every company all over the globe are minute compared to the universe and the almighty hand who created it. And on top of all that, my tiny little consulting business is insignificant compared to the entire world of business.

It makes good business sense to slow down. When I slow down, I'm more apt to truly and more accurately assess what clients need to solve their problems and meet their challenges. In business meetings, if I slow down, I will hear what others are saying more intuitively and more specifically.

> *"Wait for the Lord;*
> *Be strong, and let your heart take*
> *courage;*
> *Yes, wait for the Lord."*
>
> —Psalm 27:14, NASV

One of the hardest lessons I have had to learn as a Christian in Corporate America is how to let go of anger, and forgive people. After all, those feelings are baggage and will do nothing but weigh me down. God doesn't say to forgive when I feel like it or when I get around to it. He commands me to forgive others. When I forgive someone, I benefit so much by letting go of the weight, the baggage that's dragging me down. Letting go of baggage frees my mind to focus on providing quality goods and services to my clients. Situations or relationships that go wrong in the workplace can serve as lessons learned that help me in running my business and working on future client projects.

Some of my client relationships have gone awry. After going through the motions of being a victim, I got down to what I learned in the situations that I could apply to the future. This helped me grow as a Christian and a businessperson.

In one situation, I probably should not have accepted the work that was offered. I had an intuitive feeling during the interview process that the relationship was not going to work. Then, when I saw the contract that the client had prepared, I nearly walked away from the business at that time. When I got into the middle of the work, I found myself extremely frustrated with the situation, especially with the particular employee I was working with. I found myself being boastful in my mind about how she was so much less experienced in writing training than me. The client had not been clear with me that the woman I was working with only worked three days a week. This made scheduling meetings and moving the project forward difficult. In my effort to work as efficiently as possible, I ended up getting more and more frustrated.

I got really self-righteous in my mind about how inefficiently the client worked, which got in the way of me working efficiently. I started thinking to myself, I have worked in lots of industries, written various types of training courses and am a pretty fast writer. Excuse me, let's see if we can get my ego through the door! I went from the poor put-upon victim to a puffed up egomaniac. But, time is a healer, and finally, after several months of fussing, I looked candidly at what I did wrong; candidly at how I created my own problem by being impatient, and truthfully at the fact that not every client is a good client for me. If I had let go of my anger, perhaps I could have worked a better solution with the client. Sometimes turning work away is what I should do. If I had let go of my fear of my business not surviving, I would have made a more sound business decision in the first place.

Fear of not being able to support the family sometimes gets in the way of good business sense. That fear is related to not trusting God. Again, not letting go of control and looking to my heavenly Father for direction.

I cannot control everything and yet I can be bullheaded trying to stay in control. I say that I give all things to God, but do I really do that? I lift my open hands to the heavens and say to God, take my cares, but as I bring my hands back down, I close my fists. I take the burden back. God tells us to cast our cares on Him.

"Humble yourselves, therefore, under the mighty hand of God, that He may exalt you at the proper time, casting all your anxiety upon Him, because He cares for you."
—1 Peter 5:6-7, NASV

God has the hairs on our heads numbered and yet, we still think we can do it better then Him. Letting go is scary, but it makes sense.

"Indeed the very hairs of your head are all numbered. Do not fear; you are of more value than many sparrows."
—Luke 12:7, NASV

As I mentioned in the beginning of this book, in the description of the house, no house is perfect. No client situation is perfect either. So, we need to let go of our perfectionism so that God can do His perfect work.

My perfectionism can keep me from letting go. I won't let go of a concept with a client or I'll keep working on a piece of writing too long. I had a friend who was working on putting together a video for a high school play. As a business-owner and consultant, I can appreciate his need to make it perfect, but in this case the perfectionism kept him from finishing the project. 11 months after the play was filmed, the people who bought the videos still didn't have them.

Quality is important, but only God is absolutely perfect. We have to remember that the work and working relationships are merely God working through us. Sometimes God has to remind me that He's the one who is the author of my abilities and the successes I have.

I went to a retreat called *Amazing Grace @ Work* where it seemed that God's whole focus for me came through a dear woman that I met.

She said, "You just need to relax."

Boy was she ever right. After this retreat, rather than feeling overwhelmed with a long to-do list of how to improve my business (like I usually have when I go to a conference), I had one thing to do . . . pray that I would follow God's leading more. Now I viewed my failures differently. Ann can't really do anything, but God in Ann can do amazing things. The apostle Paul stated it perfectly.

"I can do all things through Him who strengthens me."

—Philippians 4:13, NASV

Carrying the Cross into the Workplace

God can come into our presence at work if we just invite Him. When I started my banking career at a bank in San Antonio, Texas, I had several Christian girlfriends who wanted to meet for prayer. One of my friends worked for the president of the bank, a devout Christian. He allowed us to meet in his conference room early on one morning each week to pray. Meeting with co-workers to thank God for His rich blessings and petition Him for our needs, even to come into our midst at work was a great way to start a day and a job. It seems like a miracle to me that I would get my first job out of college in a bank where the president was even willing to let us use his office space to pray.

A friend told me a story about several miracles that occurred as a result of a Support Group that he held at his office once a week. The group uses scripture as a basis for discussion and direction. My friend and his group were studying the 24th chapter of Genesis where Eliezor was sent by Abraham to find a wife for Isaac. My friend explained the story in terms of pressure on Eliezor to please his present boss by finding a wife for Isaac and pleasing his future boss since he would work for Isaac when Abraham died. Eliezor cried in desperation to God to help him with this task. He prayed that the right woman would answer him in a specific way when he talked to her. When the women approached him, he asked the question, and the one who answered the question in the way He had asked God to make her answer was Rebekah.

> *"Behold, I am standing by the spring,*
> *and the daughters of the men of the city*
> *are coming out to draw water; now may*
> *it be that the girl to whom I say, 'Please*
> *let down your jar so that I may drink,'*
> *and who answer, 'Drink and I will*
> *water your camels also'; may she be the*
> *one whom Thou hast appointed for Thy*
> *servant Isaac; and by this I shall know*
> *that Thou hast shown loving kindness to*
> *my master."*
>
> —Genesis 24:13-14, NASV

My friend suggested to the group that they each cry out their prayers during the week for God to truly meet their needs. The next week the group told some incredible stories of how God heard and answered their desperate cries. One woman had received a warning that she was going to be fired. The job at this particular firm was a second job for her; she and her husband were financially strapped at the time, so she could not afford to lose the job. God answered her with a performance review that resulted in a raise.

A second member of the group cried in desperation regarding his wife, a medical school resident, who had just had a baby when she discovered that she had Multiple Sclerosis. His wife was tired all the time and suffering from depression.

He made his cry of desperation in his backyard, as he looked skyward, "Lord, show me how to help my wife."

As he opened the sliding glass door, God told him to make the coffee so that his wife could just turn it on. The next day, as he was driving home from work, he had this uncontrollable urge to turn in at the grocery store. He told the group that God had shown him that helping his wife in small ways would make a great big difference to her.

The third person in the group reported that she was single, a bit lonely and would spend all her free time decorating cakes and watching TV. Her cry was for a purpose in life. She called a friend she had not thought of in a while. It turns out the friend needed to hear from her.

The next day, this woman's brother, who she had not heard from in months, called and asked her for advice. The most powerful call came from her ex-sister-in-law, who had remarried and found that her daughter, the woman's niece, was not getting along with the new step-siblings, could the girl live with her? The woman had found God's unique and special purpose in her life: to care for her niece. Indeed God's answers served to build the faith of the people in the group.

This same friend told of a man who was his client. The man stopped in this stock brokerage firm to sell some stock he had. My friend suggested that he could trade the stock more economically at a discount broker, but the man said he wanted to go ahead and sell the stock through my friend because he might need some other investment advice.

My friend, who rarely does this, said, "Financial investments are important, but what is even more important is an investment in your eternal life."

The man cupped his head in his hands and said, "God told you to say that." The man said he had been estranged from God and needed to get back to Him.

When my friend told him that Max Lucado is the pastor of his church, the man exclaimed, "Max Lucado! I see his books everywhere."

On reflection, my friend said that the man did not come to sell stock, God wanted him to talk to my friend so he could come home to his heavenly Father.

At one time, I worked for a consulting firm. One of my biggest clients was a bank. After two years of serving the client, the bank approached me to offer a full time position as a sales trainer and coach. I thought this was really great because the man who hired me seemed really upbeat and committed to encouraging the sales culture in the company. What I did not discover until I got to the bank was a culture steeped in back-biting, stress and unethical behavior. I was angry so much of the time when I worked there. I did not realize until later how angry I was while I worked there. The job affected my whole family. Finally after working there for two and a half years, I realized that I had to leave because I was in constant torment over expectations and ways of doing business that violated what I believed to be right. I found myself being expected to manipulate people by questioning their integrity, which was not only difficult for me, it violated my sense that God calls me to act in love toward people.

Toward the end of my time at this bank job, my boss, who lived in Houston (I lived in Dallas), had to be in Dallas for a meeting and it happened to be on Ash Wednesday. A devout Episcopalian, he asked if he could attend church with my family. As we were kneeling beside each other, humble before God, I realized that I had not had a Christian attitude toward him, that I had fallen into behaviors that I so despised. I knew then that I had to leave the job with the bank. Knowing this made the decision to take the opportunity to start my own consulting practice an easy one.

Even though that bank job was stressful, it certainly helped me grow as a person and helped me learn how to assert myself. The job also taught me how to be quiet, since often it was best to listen to all sides of a story and all the facts before stating my opinion. This helped me a lot when I continued in my own consulting practice, since listening is one of the key skills for successful consultants. What on the outside seemed like a horrible experience did affect me positively on the inside since it helped me grow. What looked like a good company to work for on the outside, on the inside had a very difficult working environment. I could have carried the cross into the workplace a lot more than I did. Unfortunately, I got caught up in the negative attitudes and behaviors. My need to succeed, my goal-driven nature got in the way of stepping back and trying to see how to bring God into the situation. I probably would have enjoyed my time at the company a whole lot more, if I had tried to bring the Lord into work situations more often. Then, I would not have been constantly torn between what I know in my heart is a right way to treat people and what I saw going on. When one boss at this particular job challenged me for agreeing too much, I could have asked him to explain his reasoning, acted like the consultant I had been training to be. Perhaps, then, he would have seen that agreeing with other departments was about achieving mutual goals. We actually might have had a better working relationship.

Though carrying Christ's cross into the workplace can seem unnerving or scary, God will honor our commitment to Him. Even if we cannot see the good of the situation at first, in the long term, carrying the cross into the workplace is the right thing to do.

Beautiful Gardens

Jesus instructed his disciples about how different people respond to the gospel. Think about how it related to sowing seeds or sharing the gospel in today's workplace.

> *"Listen to this! Behold, the sower went out to sow;*
> *And it came about that as he was sowing, some seed fell beside the road, and the birds came and ate it up.*
> *And other seed fell on the rocky ground where it did not have much soil; and immediately it sprang up because it had no depth of soil.*
> *And after the sun had risen, it was scorched; and because it had no root, it withered away.*
> *And other seed fell among the thorns, and the thorns grew up and choked it, and it yielded no crop.*

And other seeds fell into the good soil
and as they grew up and increased, they
were yielding a crop and were
producing thirty, sixty, and a
hundredfold.
And He was saying, "He who has ears
to hear, let him hear."

—Mark 4:3-9, NASV

In our attempts to make a workplace a beautiful garden and to sow seeds of faith, not all will accept what we have to share or what we demonstrate. It's not up to us to make their faith grow, just to plant the seed. When we create our gardens at home, we plant, water, fertilize to start things going, but God is really the one who makes things grow and blossom. The same is true for the people we share our faith with. Each person's faith and growth as a Christian is his or her own responsibility, and God will nurture that growth.

"I planted, Apollos watered, but God
was causing the growth.
So then, neither the one who plants nor
the one who waters is anything, but God
who causes the growth.
Now he who plants and he who waters
are one; but each will receive his own
reward according to his own labor.
For we are God's fellow-workers; you
are God's field, God's building."

—I Corinthians 3:6-9, NASV

In planting gardens, the gardener must be concerned with the right type of soil, the placement of plants, the right amount of water, irrigation of water in the flowerbeds, and the right amount of sunlight to make a garden grow. When he's planting a garden, he may have to carefully move a plant that isn't taking to the soil. New plants need plant food, to help them flourish and lots of water until their roots take hold. Different types of plants belong in different places in the garden depending on the soil, amount of water and sunlight.

The right placement and health of plants in a garden is similar to the health and well being of Christians in the workplace. Each one will flourish in the best place suited for his or her gifts and talents. A person who is great with people could use that ability as a manager or in a public relations position. Gifted writers should be in jobs where they can use that gift. Good listeners could use that skill to make terrific counselors. All the varying workers with various talents and abilities work together to make a wonderful and functioning garden with coordinated colors, seasonal blooms and pleasing symmetrical patterns.

Like new plants in the soil, new Christians need nurture too. New Christians may need help getting settled or reconciling their beliefs and value systems with daily events in their jobs. Sometimes more mature Christians need to take on the role of gardener. Gently protecting the new Christian from the wiles of Corporate life, perhaps guiding a person in the right direction. Like the gardener, you can coddle your brothers or sisters in Christ, making sure they have to right amount of sunlight in the form of guidance from you or a church. The right soil to grow in, in the form of interactions with them, will create an environment where they can grow as Christians no matter what is set in front of them in the business world. We plan for helping new Christians at church with special classes and Bible study, and yet sometimes we forget to help them forge ahead in the working world as new Christians.

We can help them by using our gifts to serve the greater needs of a team or company. We can demonstrate the resilient joy of a Christian even when things aren't going so well. Showing that we rejoice in the negative as well as the positive serves as a witness to the true joyfulness of a committed Christian life. That isn't to say that we gloss over those tough intellectual and emotional struggles that come in anyone's personal or business life, it is to say that our attitude about dealing with those tough times is driven by the knowledge that our heavenly Father will always take care of us. The garden is dependent on a skilled gardener who chooses the right plants, tends to the garden and places plants in exactly the right places. All the glory for the beautiful garden goes to the gardener. The same is true with giving God glory for what we achieve at work. For if He were not there to provide for our gifts and talents and watch over us, we would be nothing. We would wilt and die, the same way a new plant will wilt and die if the gardener does not tend to it correctly.

Gifts and Talents in the Workplace

God has given us all gifts and talents that He commands that we use to serve each other.

> *"As each one has received a gift, employ it in serving one another, as good stewards of the manifold grace of God."*
>
> —1 Peter 4:10, NASV

We are stewards of the wonderful gifts God has given us. Our gifts don't even belong to us; they belong to God. God has given each one of us a unique blend of gifts, so we can use them together to support the body of Christ. Our unique set of gifts allows us to perform the function and take the place in life to which God has called us. Those who hear and follow God's calling for them early probably wander less in the corporate jungles.

Personally, because I need variety and new challenges, I have had much more job stability as a consultant owning my own business than I ever had in a corporate job. God has given me certain analytical gifts that a variety of clients require. Each experience I have in business prepares me for the next consulting or speaking job.

Gifts and talents that God has given us are beautiful in their presentation and functional in their value. In a house, the fixtures reflect the family or the people who live in the house. The faucet has a function of providing water from the water main, yet the look and presentation of the faucet reflects who the people are, and what their tastes are. In the same way, the gifts God has given us represent who He made us to be and what our purpose for Him is. The gifts and talents that people have can be the very framework of teams in the corporation.

In the workplace, when people are using their gifts, people on teams can complement their teammate's abilities. Workers will be happier because they will be doing things they are naturally good at. And a team will function so much better if one team member does not think of himself as better than the others. This was something that Paul said about the body of Christ and the specific gifts of each member serving the community or the team in this case.

> *"For I say through the grace given to me, to everyone who is among you, not to think of himself more highly than he ought to think, but to think soberly as God has dealt to each one a measure of faith. For as we have many members in one body, but all the members do not have the same function, so we being many are one body of Christ, and individually members of one another."*
> —Romans 12:3-5, NKJV

As a consultant, I focus on sales and personal motivation. If I tried to be a technical trainer, I would not be as effective, because my skill is focused around molding behavior and attitudes to help people sell more. I wouldn't necessarily be very good at helping a database programmer write better computer code. I am more suited to help him communicate to others who don't understand what he is doing, to clearly convey a message to non-technical people in the company.

God has given us all gifts and talents that He commands that we use to serve each other.

Not only does God call us to use our gifts and talents, He has a calling for us. Recently, I visited with a man who was looking at changing careers after taking time off to handle his mother's estate. He had been a very successful salesman and knew he was good at communicating with people. He told me he was especially good at convincing people or customers to buy things that they didn't necessarily need. This knowledge plagued him for many years and now he was considering using his gift of communication in a different way. He said that gifts and talents are one thing, but what God calls you to do is another. God may call one great communicator to a career in sales and another to a life of writing, another to public speaking.

What is God calling you to do? Is it writing beautiful poetry to turn people's hearts to God? Is it selling life insurance to give people peace of mind about protecting their families? Perhaps God has called you to serve as a visionary and savvy Bank president or sharp, inspiring college professor or teacher. If you are not sure what God has called you to do, stop and pray about it, ask others to pray with you, then, listen to hear what God guides you to do.

Rejoice in the Lord Always

"It was the best of times, it was the worst of times," if how Charles Dickens started a *Tale of Two Cities*. In the end of 2001, in the United States, we found ourselves as a nation and as a community of nations, in that place.

Terrorist attacks in two cities, New York City and Washington, D.C. in the Fall of 2001 first left us stunned, vulnerable, angry, then, resolved, patriotic and faithful. The worst attack on American soil, the two towering pillars of steel, crashing to earth in a puff of smoke and ash left us staring at the unbelievable horror. We wouldn't even truly know the extent of the loss of human life until weeks later. Brothers lost sisters, moms lost sons, kids lost parents, and friends lost friends. We watched the stock market teeter, companies pushed over the edge, and many people lose their jobs. It looked like the worst of times.

Many people turned to their faith, to a faithful God in Heaven, not even necessarily to ask Him "why?" but to help them through their sorrow and shock, to move them forward to continue on with life.

Once we were safe in our lack of vulnerability, resting in the arms of a prosperous and pumped-up economy and a technology boom and bust, we had superficial worries. Many bright and able people became millionaires long before their time. Millions of dollars were thrown at dot-coms that didn't have a prayer, but had innovators who knew how to get money from their investors. It was easy to thank God for our prosperity.

Then one bright September morning, brilliant sunlight turned to darkness with ashen and choking air. Buildings weren't attacked, a way of believing, a way of faith, individual freedoms were attacked. A spiritual war was perpetrated on the United States, a war that we have fought in order to preserve the innocence of human civilian life. A war we have fought in order to preserve our right to worship and live freely with God as our director, our compass, our primary reason for everything we do.

As Christians we do not believe we must prove that we deserve eternal life, rather we know that by grace, and only grace do we receive eternal life. We find it hard to comprehend suicide bombers thinking of eternal bliss after the crash. In spite of the devastation, we can always rejoice in our promise of salvation and eternal life when we have accepted Christ in our hearts. We are called by our Lord to love our enemies, to walk in love, as Christ loved us.

> *"Therefore be imitators of God, as beloved children; and walk in love, just as Christ also loved us, and gave Himself up for us, an offering and a sacrifice to God as a fragrant aroma."*
> —Ephesians 5:1-2, NASV

Many articles, news shows, and specials have only begun to show us the expanse of the devastation, the far-reaching effects of despair, the profound changes to how we will live in the future. Even survivors have guilt that they were spared and someone else was not. And yet, the message that truly surfaces above the sorrow, is resolve, courage, and love. Families of victims show thankfulness to those who care, who pay tribute to their loved ones. We all laud heroes who lost their lives trying to save others, who worked tirelessly in a mountain of rubble, to clean up and start over. Legislators of different political ideologies put their differences aside and sang for us in harmony. Volunteers donated time, drove countless miles to help, gave resources, talents and money for the sake of helping victims.

We have started to understand and look at other parts of the world where war and terrorism have been a way of life. Some people live every day knowing that a mine, a suicide bomber or other sabotage can happen anywhere, anytime, to anyone. We have begun to see how lucky we are to live in a nation of freedom.

We can rejoice in God's grace in spite of the loss, the sorrow, but it's one of the hardest callings we will ever have. It is a calling to look at our great and precious God instead of at the devastation. Look to your God for help rather than cry out and scream about the horrible events and how they have affected our lives.

We can be thankful for people, who, on that Tuesday, were late to work or were out of their offices at the World Trade Center. We can rejoice in the lives that were spared, the heroes who continue to work tirelessly and those who knew they were going to die anyway, so they thwarted a terrorist attack and flew a plane into the ground.

Though the events of September 11, 2001 leave an indelible mark on our souls, we can see how God has triumphed over the devastation. Here is a time when God has called us to rejoice in Him, even when we didn't feel like it. In all of it, we as Christians must rejoice in the Lord always, for we cannot see God's plan. Even when we believe it's the worst of times, perhaps it's only temporary, or necessary to get to the best of times.

> *"Rejoice in the Lord always, and again I say rejoice."*
>
> —Philippians 4:4, NASV

All Things Come of Thee, Oh Lord

Could it be that God is in control of the bounty of a company? What about companies that are profitable, that totally revile God? I believe all things come from our Father in Heaven, whether we acknowledge them or not. I've seen people very close to me who have always done well in business, and in life, and always seemed to be in control, yet while they were moving along and up the ladder or being more successful, they forgot about God and His blessings. Then business started to turn devastatingly downward, family issues of great consequence arose, hearts suddenly turned to God. As though God had to get their attention. For those who know Him personally, we must remember to give Him credit for our blessings. Giving God credit will serve as a witness to people who do not know God and the richness of his blessing.

Often it's harder for strong, "together" individuals to give God credit. We are so sure we can do things that we forget who is really in charge.

I find in my own life that the minute I get all pumped up about what a terrific consultant I am, God reminds me that I am who I am and have accomplished what I have accomplished because of Him. The more I turn and truly focus on Him and give Him the credit, the better I do.

This is not to say that God never prunes me as the vinedresser prunes the grapevines. Pruning makes me stronger though, and more able to handle what life puts in front of me. Bruce Wilkinson, in his book *The Secrets of the Vine,* gives great stories and explanations for how and why God prunes us. When we bear better fruit, we are more of a witness of God's glory, power and ultimate control in our lives. When we acknowledge that all things come from God, it takes pressure off of us so we can relax and share God's love and peace with others. By giving God credit, and looking to Him for strength and our every need we can focus on Him instead of all the turmoil and insanity around us in the world.

A college friend once told me, "God doesn't always send what we want, but He does always give us what we need." That thought has helped me quite a bit through my business life. For example, my business was going extremely well for the first three years, then I moved to a different town and my revenue dropped by 40 percent. I *wanted* my business to prosper like it had, what I *needed* was humility. Humility to trust God, humility to follow His blueprint for the house He is building rather than the house I wanted to build.

He knows what we need and will send it our way. Sometimes what we need is different than what we want. In building a house, the homebuilder may advise a potential owner, who wants a three-car garage, that perhaps what he needs is a two-car garage to leave more space to create rooms in the house. The homeowner may not exactly like the answer but it is truly what the homeowner needs. Like the builder who tells an owner that it will take six months to build the house he wants.

The owner may say, "Well, I want it in four, because I'm having a big party."

If the builder were to cut corners to build it in four for the party, it might not turn out to be such a great party if all the walls started falling down.

So many times in my business, I have been ready to give up, when God had a different plan. He had blessing in store that I could not see. So many blessings that we can't see or imagine are waiting around the corner. The waiting and trusting Him are really a blessing to us too, because that gives us experience to know that God will not forsake us. He will constantly guide us and be steadfast to us. He has a constant fatherly nature of helping us trust Him, have faith in Him and get the right perspective. This life on earth is so temporary anyway, Our time on earth waiting for our savior to come take us home is short, the snap of a finger, compared to eternity. Our riches and reward are in Heaven, eternally with our heavenly Father.

> *"Instruct those who are rich in this*
> *present world not to be conceited or to*
> *fix their hope on the uncertainty of*
> *riches, but on God, who richly supplies*
> *us with all things to enjoy."*
> —1 Timothy 6:17, NASV

It's like a colleague of mine said, "If you look up, you get up, if you look down, all you see is brown dirt."

We must look up and thank Him for all He has sent and all His many blessings. We must raise our hearts toward our Father who blesses us with all things in this life, whether we like them or not.

> *"Seek ye first the kingdom of God and*
> *all these things will be added unto*
> *you."*
> —Matthew 6:33, NASV

Living in the Neighborhood — The Weak Shall Lead the Strong

"Blessed are the poor in spirit, for theirs is the kingdom of heaven. Blessed are they that mourn, for they shall be comforted. Blessed are the meek, for they shall inherit the earth. Blessed are those who hunger and thirst after righteousness, for they shall be filled. Blessed are the merciful, for they shall obtain mercy. Blessed are the pure in heart, for they shall see God. Blessed are the peacemakers, for they shall be called the children of God. Blessed are those who are persecuted for righteousness sake, for theirs is the kingdom of Heaven."

—Matthew 5:3-10, NKJV

One of the most revered spiritual leaders of our time was Mother Teresa. She died with few possessions, yet left an indelible impression on our society. A quiet, yet strong-spoken woman of incredible compassion and faith, she was a meek, merciful peacemaker, pure in heart.

If you bring God into the workplace, do you have the risk of being ridiculed or treated with less respect? Might you be persecuted for righteousness sake? Will it stop you from sharing your faith, the faithfulness of your savior or the glory of serving Him? Sometimes you have to come across as the weak one to really be the strong one. You may have to be merciful to someone who you might otherwise shun. Know that whatever God calls you to do in the workplace, however you go out on a limb for Him, He will honor.

Wherever you are, whatever you are doing, you can always know there is a loving, almighty and gracious God at work.

CPSIA information can be obtained at www.ICGtesting.com
Printed in the USA
236292LV00004B/1/P